"These books t   ⅃
throughout the   ⊃
a thought-provoking, vision-expanu...y, p r-
stimulating tool. These books are small enough to
fit into your pocket, but big enough to change your
life. Simple, but brilliant."

Dr Sinclair B. Ferguson, Ligonier teaching fellow
and Professor of Systematic Theology,
Westminster Theological Seminary

"We watch the news, read articles, and hear stories
about difficulties in our world. The needs are so
massive, the stories so heartbreaking, that often we
don't even know how to pray. Rachel Jones's excel-
lent book, *5 Things to Pray for Your World*, offers a
needed guide to seek God's help by praying God's
word. We may feel powerless, but we have the ear
of an all-powerful God. May we faithfully cry out to
him for the world around us."

Melissa Kruger, author, *The Envy of Eve* and
Walking with God in the Season of Motherhood

"Praying God's word is my number one tip to help
people invigorate their prayer life. So read these
books and invigorate your prayers."

Tim Chester, Pastor of Grace Church,
Boroughbridge, faculty member of Crosslands
Training, and author of *You Can Pray*

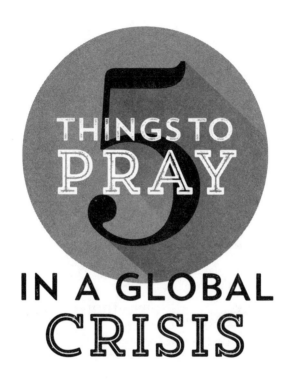

THINGS TO
5
PRAY

IN A GLOBAL
CRISIS

RACHEL JONES
SERIES EDITOR: CARL LAFERTON

5 things to pray in a global crisis
Prayers that change things in times of trouble
© The Good Book Company, 2020.
Series Editor: Carl Laferton

Published by:
The Good Book Company

thegoodbook.com | www.thegoodbook.co.uk
thegoodbook.com.au | thegoodbook.co.nz | thegoodbook.co.in

Unless indicated, all Scripture references are taken from the Holy
Bible, New International Version. Copyright © 2011 Biblica, Inc.
Used by permission.

ISBN: 9781784985707 | Printed in the USA

Design by André Parker

CONTENTS

PRAYING FOR MY CHURCH

PRAYING FOR KINGDOM GROWTH

INTRODUCTION

We are living in literally extraordinary times—times that will permanently shape us, our families and our nations. The COVID-19 pandemic has shown us that, even in the 21st-century Western world, life is fragile, wealth is fleeting and plans are easily disrupted.

In other words, we are living in the same world that James wrote about in his letter to our first-century spiritual ancestors (read James 4 v 14; 1 v 10; 4 v 13, 15). And what does James urge God's people to do when crises come? "Is anyone among you in trouble? Let them pray" (5 v 13). Why? Because—and here is a verse to cling to in times of trouble:

> *"The prayer of a righteous person is powerful and effective." (James 5 v 16)*

James is telling us that when righteous people pray righteous prayers, things happen. Things change. The prayers of God's people are *powerful*. They are not powerful because we are powerful, or because the words we say are somehow magic, but because the Person we pray to is infinitely, unimaginably powerful. And our prayers are *effective*—not because we are special, or because there is a special formula to use, but because the God we pray to delights to answer our prayers and change the world because of them.

So what is the secret of effective prayer during the coronavirus crisis? How can you pray prayers that really change things? James suggests two questions that we need to ask ourselves.

First, are you righteous? A righteous person is someone who is in right relationship with God—someone who, through faith in Jesus, has been forgiven and accepted as a child of God. Are you someone who, as you pray, is praying not just to your Maker, not just to your Ruler, but to your heavenly Father, who has completely forgiven you through Jesus?

Second, do your prayers reflect that relationship? If we know God is our Maker, our Ruler and our Father, we will want to pray prayers that please him, that reflect his desires, and that line up with his priorities for our lives and for the world. The kind of prayer that truly changes things is the prayer offered by a child of God that reflects God's heart.

That's why, when God's children pray in the Bible, we so often find them using the word of God to guide their prayers. So when Jonah prayed in the belly of a fish to thank God for rescuing him (Jonah 2 v 1-9), he used the words of several psalms strung together. When the first Christians gathered in Jerusalem to pray, they used the themes of Psalm 2 to guide their praise and their requests (Acts 4 v 24-30). And when Paul prayed that his friends would grow in love (Philippians 1 v 9), he was asking the Father to work in them the same thing the Lord Jesus prayed for us (John 17 v 25-26), and which the Holy Spirit is doing for all believers (Romans 5 v 5). They all used God's words to guide their words to God.

Many of us have been prompted to pray more by the crisis we are living through. But equally, many of us are unsure precisely *how* to pray and what to ask. How can you pray prayers that are powerful and effective—that change things? First, by being a child of God. Second, by praying Bible prayers, which use God's words, to make sure that your prayers are pleasing to him and share his priorities.

That's what this little book is here to help you with. It will guide you on how to pray about 21 different aspects of life during this pandemic—how to pray well for yourself, your loved ones and your church… for the response in your nation and across the world… and for God's kingdom. Not all the prayers will be relevant to your particular personal situation all the time—but where that is the case, you can use them to pray for others who are facing the situation being addressed.

Each prayer suggestion is based on a passage of the Bible, so you can be certain that they are prayers that God wants you to pray at this time.

There are five different things to pray for each of the 21 areas. So you can use this book in a variety of ways.

- ▶ *You can pray a set of "five things" each day, over the course of three weeks, and then start again.*

- ▶ *You can take one of the prayer themes and pray a part of it every day from Monday to Friday.*

- *Or you can dip in and out of it as and when you want and need to pray about a particular aspect of this crisis.*

- *There's also a space on each page for you to write in the names of specific situations, concerns or people that you intend to remember in prayer.*

This is by no means an exhaustive guide. But you can be confident as you use it that you are praying prayers that God wants you to pray. And God promises that "the prayer of a righteous person is powerful and effective". That's a promise that is worth grasping hold of confidently. As we pray trusting this promise, it will change how we pray and what we expect to come from our prayers.

When righteous people pray righteous prayers, things happen. Things change. God is powerful; and so your prayers are too.

Carl Laferton
EVP Publishing | The Good Book Company

THINGS TO
PRAY
5

PRAYING FOR...

PEACE WHEN I AM ANXIOUS

PSALM 23

PRAYER POINTS:

_____

_____

_____

_____

Father in heaven, help me to trust that you are…

 ## MY GOOD SHEPHERD

*"The LORD is my shepherd, I lack nothing"
(v 1).*

There are lots of reasons to feel afraid and vulnerable right now. But praise God that you are a sheep with a good shepherd. He knows you, and loves you, and is committed to caring for you. Thank him for the good things he's given you—the "green pastures" and "quiet waters", which show his kindness (v 2). Thank the Lord Jesus for being a shepherd who laid down his life to provide all that is needed for the salvation of his sheep.

 ## GUIDING ME

*"He refreshes my soul. He guides me along
the right paths for his name's sake" (v 3).*

Perhaps you are worried about a decision or are unsure how to help someone you love—ask God to guide you. Then ask him to use this time to make you ever more prayerful. Pray that as you spend time with him in his word each day, he would refresh your soul.

LEADING ME THROUGH

> *"Even though I walk through the darkest valley, I will fear no evil, for you are with me" (v 4).*

Anxiety feels like a valley that we see no way out of—but our shepherd has promised to lead us through to the other side. Ask God to calm your fears and bless you with a real sense of his presence. Then pray the same for any people who you're worried about.

 WITH ME TOMORROW

> *"Surely your goodness and love will follow me all the days of my life..." (v 6).*

Jesus' words are apt for this crisis: "Do not worry about tomorrow, for tomorrow will worry about itself. Each day has enough trouble of its own" (Matthew 6 v 34). Ask for his help to take things one day at a time, knowing that whatever you face when you wake up tomorrow—and on every day that follows—God's goodness and love are assured and his grace is sufficient.

 MY SHEPHERD ETERNALLY

> *"... and I will dwell in the house of the LORD for ever" (v 6).*

Thank God that because you are one of Jesus' sheep, you will spend eternity dwelling with him, in perfect security and peace. Pray that knowing this would help you not to fear sickness or death, but instead to live with growing joy and confidence.

PRAYING FOR...

COMFORT WHEN I AM LONELY

PSALM 139

PRAYER POINTS:

_____

_____

_____

_____

Father, when I am lonely, help me to remember...

 ## YOU KNOW ME

> *"You have searched me, LORD, and you know me. You know when I sit and when I rise" (v 1-2).*

Loneliness is so hard to endure. But praise God that, even when we feel at our most alone and unknown, he sees us and understands us perfectly. It may be that no one else can share in what we're doing or see how we're feeling, but God is "familiar with all [our] ways" (v 3). So talk to him now—out loud if that helps—about whatever is on your heart.

 ## YOUR SPIRIT IS WITH ME

> *"Where can I go from your Spirit? Where can I flee from your presence?" (v 7).*

God isn't just "out there" looking down on us—he dwells *within us* by his Spirit. Thank him for this truth, and ask him to graciously give you an increasing awareness of his Spirit's presence. Pray that in this season of isolation you'll walk closely with him day by day.

YOUR HOPE

> *"Even the darkness will not be dark to you; the night will shine like the day, for darkness is as light to you" (v 12).*

Loneliness can make us feel very low. Ask God to help you to hold on to the gospel hope—that Jesus, the light of the world, has come and is coming again soon.

 YOUR SOVEREIGNTY

> *"All the days ordained for me were written in your book before one of them came to be" (v 16).*

One of the hardest things is not knowing how long this is going to last, or when we'll be able to see our loved ones again. But praise God: he does know! These are not wasted days but ones ordained by him for our good. Pray for a growing sense of awe at his sovereignty.

 YOUR CALL TO LOVE OTHERS

> *"See if there is any offensive way in me, and lead me in the way everlasting" (v 24).*

In a situation like this it is so easy to become inward-looking or to give in to self-pity. Humbly ask God to show you whether there are any ways in which you might be responding to your circumstances sinfully. Pray that in each day of isolation you will still be looking to love and serve others—perhaps by praying for them or by calling to encourage them. Start by praying for the needs of some people you know now.

PRAYING FOR...

WISDOM WHEN I AM UNCERTAIN

PROVERBS 3 v 1-12

PRAYER POINTS:

_____

_____

_____

_____

Whether we're weighing up risks or trying to plan for the future in the midst of uncertainty, we need wisdom. So ask God to help you to...

 REMEMBER HIS WORD

"My son, do not forget my teaching, but keep my commands in your heart" (v 1).

Thank God for the ways that he has prepared you for this situation—for all the things you have learned from his word and from his people over the years. Pray that you would remember the Lord's certain "love and faithfulness" (v 3) in the coming weeks and act with love and faithfulness towards others.

 TRUST IN HIM

"Trust in the LORD with all your heart and lean not on your own understanding" (v 5).

How quick we are to feel self-sufficient! Thank God for using this situation to reveal your need of his wisdom. Ask him to help you to prayerfully trust him, and not yourself, with all your heart. Pray too that no part of you would give way to anxiety, and that you would be able to rest well as you entrust all things to him.

WALK HIS PATHS

"In all your ways submit to him, and he will make your paths straight" (v 6).

Ask for grace to submit to all God's commands and providences. Pray that you would not be paralysed by indecision, but that he would help you to move forward in faith, trusting that he will make your paths straight and work all things for your eternal good.

HONOUR HIM FINANCIALLY

"Honour the LORD with your wealth" (v 9).

The economic impact of this crisis is bound to affect all of us in one way or another. Whether you have a lot or a little when it comes to money, pray that your greatest desire would be to honour God with all of the resources he has given you. Ask for his help to make wise decisions as you plan your spending in the future—not motivated by fear but seeking to be both prudent and generous.

DISCERN YOUR DISCIPLINE

"Do not despise the LORD's discipline ... because the LORD disciplines those he loves" (v 11-12).

Sometimes God uses our circumstances to show us the things we are holding too tightly and the sins we are taking too lightly. How might he be doing that at the moment? Ask him to help you to respond to his loving discipline and to change your ways accordingly.

PRAYING FOR...

PATIENCE WHEN I AM FRUSTRATED

JAMES 5 v 7-11

_____

_____

_____

_____

 PATIENT FOR CHRIST'S COMING

> *"Be patient, then, brothers and sisters, until the Lord's coming ... be patient and stand firm" (v 7-8).*

It's easy to grow frustrated as we wait for this all to be over. Yet in many ways, the Christian life is one long waiting game—we're waiting for Christ to return to put our world to rights. At a time like this we may doubt if that day will ever come. So ask God to make you patient. Pray for perseverance to stand firm in your faith for as long as it takes for Jesus to return.

 PATIENT WITH MY WORDS

> *"Don't grumble against one another, brothers and sisters, or you will be judged" (v 9).*

Confess the times that you have grumbled against other people in the last few days—to their face, behind their back, or in your heart. Ask God to help you to be patient with others today, and to be gracious and grateful in your words and attitude.

PATIENT IN MY WITNESS

"As an example of patience in the face of suffering, take the prophets who spoke in the name of the Lord" (v 10).

Pray that in this season of suffering, you wouldn't give up trying to "speak in the name of the Lord". Pray that you would speak boldly of Jesus, even when it's costly.

 PATIENT WITH GOD

"As you know, we count as blessed those who have persevered. You have heard of Job's perseverance and have seen what the Lord finally brought about" (v 11).

"Why is God letting this happen?" "When will he stop this?" "Why won't he answer my prayers?" Ask God to help you to be patient with his plans, and specifically with their timing. Pray for increasing confidence that God's ways always lead to blessing for his people, even when you can't see how that can be.

 PATIENT LIKE GOD

"The Lord is full of compassion and mercy" (v 11).

Thank God for how patient he is with you. When you are weak, he shows you compassion. When you are sinful, he shows you mercy. Thank him for specific ways in which you have experienced his patience recently, and pray that you would show the same compassion and mercy to those around you today.

PRAYING FOR...

CONFIDENCE WHEN I AM CONFUSED

ISAIAH 55 v 1-13

PRAYER POINTS:

_____

_____

_____

_____

"Why is God letting this happen?" A crisis can raise all sorts of doubts and questions. Ask God to give you confidence that he is real and that his ways are...

 GENEROUS

> *"Come, all you who are thirsty, come to the waters ... come, buy and eat!" (v 1).*

In the face of all that we don't know, it's wise to keep coming back to what we *do*: God is good. Thank him for his generosity, demonstrated most clearly in the gift of his Son, who declared, "Let anyone who is thirsty come to me and drink" (John 7 v 37). Praise him!

 MERCIFUL

> *"Let [the wicked] turn to the LORD, and he will have mercy on them" (v 7).*

All is not right in the world because all is not right with people: we have collectively turned away from our Creator and are all living with the consequences of a world broken by sin. So confess your sins and acknowledge the brokenness of your society. Rejoice in God's mercy to you and ask him to extend his mercy to your nation and to your neighbours.

HIGHER

"As the heavens are higher than the earth,
so are my ways higher than your ways and
my thoughts than your thoughts" (v 9).

Admit to God the truth of this verse: he doesn't run the world in the way that you would, and that is a good thing. Tell him about the doubts you're struggling with, and ask him to help you to trust him with them.

 ### PURPOSEFUL

"[My word] will not return to me empty, but
will accomplish what I desire and achieve
the purpose for which I sent it" (v 11).

We may not know exactly *what* God is doing through this crisis, but we can be confident that he is doing *something*. Where have you seen his word bear fruit in the midst of it (in the lives of his people or not-yet Christians)? Praise God for this evidence of his word at work and ask him for the privilege of seeing more.

 ### ETERNALLY GLORIOUS

"You will go out in joy and be led forth in
peace ... This will be for the LORD's renown
... that will endure for ever" (v 12-13).

Praise God that he has promised you an eternal future of joy and peace. Ask for his help to hold on to that hope in the midst of your doubts. And pray that throughout this crisis, your greatest longing would be not to know all the answers but for God to be glorified.

PRAYING FOR...

HOPE WHEN I AM GRIEVING

JOHN 11 v 1-44

PRAYER POINTS:

_____

_____

_____

_____

Whether you're mourning someone close to you or for the many who have died, ask God to help you to…

 ## CALL ON JESUS

"The sisters sent word to Jesus" (v 3).

In the face of the overwhelming tragedy of death, there is ultimately only one person we can turn to for help: Jesus. Perhaps you share Martha and Mary's sense of hurt and confusion as they grieved the death of their brother Lazarus: "Lord … if you had been here, my brother would not have died" (v 21, 32). So call on Jesus now and tell him honestly how you feel.

 ## SEE GOD'S GLORY

"It is for God's glory so that God's Son may be glorified through it" (v 4).

As hard as it may be to perceive right now, we know that God in his sovereignty weaves together all events to glorify his Son. Ask God to enable you to long for the glory of Jesus. Pray that he would indeed be glorified in the midst of this pain, whether or not the Lord gives you eyes to see it.

RECEIVE ETERNAL LIFE

> *"I am the resurrection and the life. The one who believes in me will live, even though they die; and whoever lives by believing in me will never die" (v 25-26).*

Pause and meditate on these wonderful words, and let them move you to praise even in the midst of grief. Thank Jesus that his resurrection guarantees the resurrection of all those who die trusting in him, including your own. Ask him to keep you believing this promise, even as you grieve.

 ### KNOW THAT JESUS CARES

> *"When Jesus saw her weeping ... he was deeply moved in spirit and troubled ... Jesus wept" (v 33, 35).*

Jesus knows how it feels to cry with grief. He sees, and he cares. Pray that this would give you comfort. Pray that all those affected by grief would come to see Jesus as we see him in this story—deeply grieved for the hurting and outraged at the intrusion of suffering into his creation—and would so come to him for comfort.

 ### WITNESS GOD'S INTERVENTION

> *"The dead man came out" (v 43).*

Just as the Father accepted his Son's prayer (v 41-42), so he accepts the prayers of his Son's people. What might it look like for God to intervene in this situation for good? Ask him to do act in that way now.

PRAYING FOR MY FAMILY

MY SPOUSE

1 PETER 3 v 8

PRAYER POINTS:

_____

_____

_____

_____

Father in heaven, please help me and my spouse to…

BE LIKE-MINDED

"Finally, all of you, be like-minded" (v 8).

This verse was first addressed to churches under pressure, but it applies equally well to families under pressure! With normal routines up in the air and uncertainties about the future, there are perhaps more opportunities than usual for differences of opinion between you and your spouse. Ask God to bless you with a real sense of unity at this time—that he would help you to pull together as you both seek to honour Jesus.

BE SYMPATHETIC

"… be sympathetic" (v 8).

In what areas is your spouse struggling at the moment? What weaknesses do they feel? What sins are they battling? What worries or responsibilities weigh them down? Ask God to help you to be sympathetic. Pray that you would patiently listen to them and lovingly pray for them—not just once or twice but for however long they struggle. (Why not start by praying now?)

3 LOVE ONE ANOTHER

"… love one another" (v 8).

"Greater love has no one than this: to lay down one's life for one's friends" (John 15 v 13). Spend some time thanking the Lord Jesus that, out of love, he laid down his life for you. Then pray that knowing this would enable you to lay down your life—your time, your energy, your preferences—for the sake of your spouse. When might you have an opportunity to do that today? Ask for God's help to take it.

 ### **4 GROW IN COMPASSION**

"… be compassionate" (v 8).

Pray that this would be a time when both you and your spouse grow in compassion—not just for one another but for those outside of your household too. Ask God to protect you from becoming inward looking (even if you're stuck indoors). Pray that you would be spurring one another on towards love and good deeds done for the sake of your church family and non-Christian neighbours (Hebrews 10 v 24).

 ### **5 HUMBLY REPENT**

"… and humble" (v 8).

Repent of times in the last few days when your pride has caused conflict. Pray that when you mess up, you would both be quick to humbly acknowledge your fault, confess your sin, extend forgiveness and receive grace—from God and from one another.

PRAYING FOR MY FAMILY

MY KIDS

PSALM 78 v 1-8

PRAYER POINTS:

_____

_____

_____

_____

Father God, please help our family to...

 ## GIVE THANKS

> *"My people, hear my teaching ... things we have heard and known, things our ancestors have told us" (v 1, 3).*

Thank God for the people he used to ensure that you can say today that you "have heard and known" about "his power, and the wonders he has done" (v 4)—especially his wonderful work of rescuing sinners through the death and resurrection of Jesus. Thank God for the privilege of making his deeds known to the next generation as they grow up in your house.

 ## SPEAK YOUR PRAISE

> *"We will tell the next generation the praiseworthy deeds of the LORD" (v 4).*

It's so easy for our kids to mainly hear us complaining and criticising! Pray instead that they would hear you praising God with an infectious sense of gratitude for answered prayers, small mercies and daily blessings—even (especially) during this time.

FORM LASTING MEMORIES

> *"He commanded our ancestors to teach their children so that ... they in turn would tell their children" (v 5-6).*

How will your kids look back on this time? One thing is sure: it will not leave them unchanged. Pray that they would be able to remember it as a time when they learned from their parents—through their words and their example—more of what it means to follow Jesus, love others, and rejoice always.

 TRUST IN GOD

> *"Then they would put their trust in God and would not forget his deeds..." (v 7).*

Pray that each of your children would not be afraid of this pandemic, but would "put their trust in God" in a new way for themselves.

 GROW IN OBEDIENCE

> *"... but would keep his commands. They would not be like their ancestors—a stubborn and rebellious generation" (v 7-8).*

New situations always bring new challenges to our obedience—whatever our age. Talk to God about some of the specific ways in which your children, and yourself, are struggling to obey him. Ask him to give your whole family supple hearts which are quick to repent and eager to obey.

THINGS TO PRAY 5

PRAYING FOR MY FAMILY

LOVED ONES I CANNOT VISIT

1 THESSALONIANS 3 v 6-13

PRAYER POINTS:

_____

_____

_____

_____

 EAGER LONGING

> *"[Timothy] has told us that you always have pleasant memories of us and that you long to see us, just as we also long to see you" (v 6).*

If we're longing to see someone, it's because we love them—and to love and be loved in return is a sweet blessing, as Paul knew when he wrote to this Thessalonian church that he was parted from. So thank God for those you love but cannot visit: for the love you have, for the "pleasant memories" you share, and for the means you have to keep in touch.

 STANDING FIRM

> *"Now we really live, since you are standing firm in the Lord. How can we thank God enough for you in return for all the joy we have in the presence of God because of you?" (v 8-9).*

Pray that this person would come to, or continue to, stand firm in the Lord—trusting in Christ for their salvation, even in the midst of difficulty. Does this person's faith put a smile on your face? Then thank God!

A WAY TO BE REUNITED

"Now may our God and Father himself and our Lord Jesus clear the way for us to come to you" (v 11).

Ask God to bring this pandemic to an end, so that you can safely see your loved one again soon.

 ## INCREASING LOVE

"May the Lord make your love increase and overflow for each other and for everyone else, just as ours does for you" (v 12).

Pray that, by God's Spirit, this person would be growing in love for their Lord, their family, their church, and their neighbours. Pray that this love would overflow in their words, deeds and prayers. Ask God to give you a deepening, more Christ-like, more selfless love for this person, even in this time apart.

 ## STRONG HEARTS

"May he strengthen your hearts so that you will be blameless and holy in the presence of our God and Father when our Lord Jesus comes with all his holy ones" (v 13).

We long for the day when we will see our friends and family again—but pray that you would long with even greater eagerness for the day when you will meet God face to face. Pray that your faith would stay strong so that you can look forward to that day with confidence, knowing that you are "blameless and holy" in Christ.

PRAYING FOR THE RESPONSE

HEALTHCARE

2 CORINTHIANS 1 v 3-11

PRAYER POINTS:

_____

_____

_____

_____

This page has been written with the help of Helen Greenfield, a medical doctor working on a ward of suspected COVID-19 cases in London.

 FATHER OF COMPASSION...

> *"Praise be to ... the Father of compassion and the God of all comfort, who comforts us in all our troubles..." (v 3-4).*

Think back to periods of ill-health when God has comforted you. Thank God that he looks at our broken world with compassion and stands ready to comfort all those who turn to him for help.

 COMFORT THOSE IN TROUBLE

> *"... so that we can comfort those in any trouble with the comfort we ourselves receive from God" (v 4).*

Pray for medical staff as they seek to comfort the sick and dying, and support one another. Ask God to give them an abundance of compassion, patience and grace. Pray that Christians working in the health service would take every opportunity to speak of the unique comfort that the gospel gives.

HELP THOSE UNDER PRESSURE

"We were under great pressure, far beyond our ability to endure … But this happened that we might not rely on ourselves but on God, who raises the dead" (v 8-9).

Pray for staff as they make difficult decisions about how to treat patients with limited resources. Ask God to give them wisdom. Pray that in this time of great pressure, many staff would come to see their own need of a Saviour who has conquered death.

 ### DELIVER MANY FROM DANGER

"He has delivered us from such a deadly peril, and he will deliver us again. On him we have set our hope…" (v 10).

Praise God that he loves to deliver people from danger, including ill-health—in his grace, he often works through the skill of medical professionals. Ask him to use doctors, nurses and others to save many lives, and to bring this pandemic to an end soon.

 ### AND ANSWER OUR PRAYERS

"… as you help us by your prayers. Then many will give thanks on our behalf for the gracious favour granted us in answer to the prayers of many" (v 11).

Give thanks for ways in which God has answered your prayers for the sick in the past. Who can you "help … by your prayers" right now?

PRAYING FOR THE RESPONSE

OUR GOVERNMENT

ROMANS 13 v 1-7

PRAYER POINTS:

_____

_____

_____

_____

 ESTABLISHED BY GOD

> *"The authorities that exist have been established by God" (v 1).*

A crisis like this shows how important a stable government is. (This situation is much worse for those who do not live under one.) The Bible teaches that government is a gift from God, for our good. So thank him for it; and thank him for your nation's leaders, by name.

 WILLING SUBMISSION

> *"Let everyone be subject to the governing authorities" (v 1).*

While many of us bristle at having our freedoms curtailed, Christians should be exemplary in the way that we follow the rules—not because we fear a social-media shaming but "as a matter of conscience", because it honours God (v 5). So ask him to help you to submit to your government's regulations at this time: willingly, completely, even joyfully. Then pray that by God's grace, your whole society would submit to authority for the sake of one another.

WORKING FOR GOOD

> *"The one in authority is God's servant for your good"* (v 4).

Pray for your government as it seeks to work for the good of your nation. Every day there are many hard decisions, with no easy answers and no guaranteed outcomes. How our leaders need God's wisdom! So ask him to grant it to them.

 LIMITING WRONG

> *"They are God's servants, agents of wrath to bring punishment on the wrongdoer"* (v 4).

Pray for the police and other authorities as they seek to enforce regulations; ask God to help them to act in a way that is measured but effective, so that the vulnerable are protected. More broadly, pray that this would not be a time when evil is able to flourish or the weak are able to be oppressed, but that God would work through human agents to uphold justice.

 OWED RESPECT

> *"Give to everyone what you owe them ... if respect, then respect; if honour, then honour"* (v 7).

Repent of any recent times when you have spoken about your leaders in a way that was disrespectful. Ask God to change your heart and to guard your mouth. Honour your leaders by praying for them by name now.

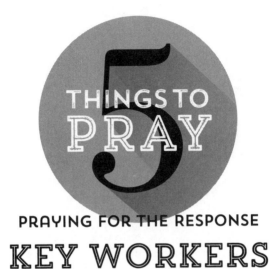

PRAYING FOR THE RESPONSE

KEY WORKERS

PROVERBS 15 v 1-33

PRAYER POINTS:

_____

_____

_____

_____

"Key workers" are those whose work is critical to the COVID-19 response (e.g. health and social care, food production and delivery, utilities, etc).

KNOWLEDGEABLE

"The eyes of the Lord are everywhere, keeping watch on the wicked and the good" (v 3).

Praise God that he is sovereign over his world. His concern is not limited to the affairs of his people—he rules over *all* people. Ask him to help you to pray confidently for the needs of your nation, knowing that he is able, and willing, to intervene.

SUCCESSFUL PLANS

"Plans fail for lack of counsel, but with many advisors they succeed" (v 22).

This crisis has demanded new and frequently changing plans across so many sectors. Pray that as people work together, their plans to work for good would succeed; and that systems would continue to function, for the sake of the common good.

PROTECTING THE VULNERABLE

"The LORD tears down the house of the proud, but he sets the widow's boundary stones in place" (v 25).

We serve a God of justice, who desires that the vulnerable members of our society will be protected. Pray that the elderly and at-risk would be able to access the help that they need, and pray for all those key workers responsible for delivering it.

 ## GOOD NEWS SOON

"Light in a messenger's eyes brings joy to the heart, and good news gives health to the bones" (v 30).

Ask God to bless the nation's key workers with good health and strong morale, even in the face of many pressures. Pray that soon we would all have the joy of sharing in the good news that this crisis is abating.

 ## LASTING HONOUR

"Wisdom's instruction is to fear the LORD, and humility comes before honour" (v 33).

It's right to honour our key workers for the part they're playing in fighting this pandemic. Thank God for them now. Yet we know that it is only those who bow the knee to King Jesus in this life who will enjoy an eternal crown in the next. So ask God to use this crisis to cause many people to fear him rightly. Pray that for any key workers you know by name.

PRAYING FOR THE RESPONSE

THOSE WHO ARE SICK

MARK 1 v 29-39

PRAYER POINTS:

_____

_____

_____

_____

 TELL JESUS

*"Simon's mother-in-law was in bed with a
fever, and they immediately told Jesus
about her" (v 30).*

Praise God that whenever someone we know falls
sick, we too can immediately tell Jesus about them.
Wherever we are, Jesus is not beyond the reach of
our prayers. He is always available and always hears
his followers when we ask him for help. He cares
about the people we care about. So tell Jesus about
the sick person who is on your mind.

 HEALING FOR THEM

*"So he went up to her, took her hand and
helped her up. The fever left her and she
began to wait on them" (v 31).*

Praise Jesus that he is the one with all authority over
every illness. Ask him to heal this person. Pray that he
would restore them to total health—that very soon
they would be able to spend their renewed strength
serving Jesus and his people.

HEALING FOR MANY

"That evening … the whole town gathered at the door, and Jesus healed many who had various diseases" (v 32-34).

For all the people known to us who are sick, there are thousands whose names we don't know. But they are not unknown to Jesus. So pray for all those suffering from illness—that God would mercifully heal many as he gives wisdom and strength to those treating them.

 ## SPIRITUAL REST

"Very early in the morning … Jesus got up, left the house and went off to a solitary place, where he prayed" (v 35).

In the midst of many pressing needs, Jesus prioritised prayer. Pray that this sick person and their family would find spiritual rest for their souls as they bring their anxieties to God in prayer.

 ## SALVATION

"Jesus replied, 'Let us go somewhere else—to the nearby villages—so that I can preach there also. That is why I have come'" (v 38).

Praise God that Jesus came not just to heal sickness but to preach a gospel that can deal with our sin. Pray that, as a result of this situation, many people would "repent and believe the good news" (1 v 15). Pray by name for specific non-Christians.

PRAYING FOR MY CHURCH

UNITY

JOHN 17 v 20-26

PRAYER POINTS:

_____

_____

_____

_____

How can a church be united while we're all separated? Ask God to help your church to...

 KNOW HIS PROTECTION

> *"I pray also for those who will believe in me through their message..." (v 20).*

Long before this pandemic started—indeed, long before any of us were born—Jesus prayed that his church would be united. Praise God for the way he has preserved his people through many challenges throughout history. Pray that this would give you confidence as you face this challenge.

 GROW IN UNITY

> *"... that all of them may be one, Father, just as you are in me and I am in you..." (v 21).*

The unity of the Father and Son is not merely a matter of them sharing the same space once a week—it's a deep, constant, unbreakable spiritual reality. The same is true of your church's bonds. Pray that this time of separation would give you all a growing sense of the way that Christ has knitted you together as family.

WITNESS TO THE WORLD

> "… so that the world may believe that you
> have sent me" (v 21).

Pray that your church's unity would be a powerful witness to unbelievers, as they see that Jesus is not a hobby that we put on hold. Think of those who were on the fringes of church life before this crisis—pray that the way that you love them and stay in touch with them would convince them of Christ's claims. Pray for chances to speak enthusiastically to non-Christians about how grateful you are to be part of Christ's church.

 LOOK FORWARD, TOGETHER

> "Father, I want those you have given me
> to be with me where I am, and to see my
> glory" (v 24).

All of us have loved ones whom we wish we could be with, physically. So does Jesus: he longs for the day when *you* and *your* church family will join him in glory. Pray that you and your brothers and sisters would stand together spiritually as you all look forward to that day.

 LOVE ONE ANOTHER

> "I … will continue to make you known [to
> them] in order that the love you have for
> me may be in them" (v 26).

Pray that as you grow in knowing God, you would grow in love for your brothers and sisters. Ask him to show you how you can love someone in your church today.

PRAYING FOR MY CHURCH

GROWTH

COLOSSIANS 1 v 9-14

PRAYER POINTS:

_____

_____

_____

_____

Paul had "not stopped praying" (v 9) for the Colossian church while he was in Rome. Pray that your church would "live a life worthy of the Lord" as you grow in...

 GOOD WORKS

"bearing fruit in every good work..." (v 10).

Church life has changed—but what has not changed is the opportunity to love others! Pray that as a church you would be living out your faith as you serve your families, work hard in your jobs, care for your neighbours, and pray for and encourage one another.

 KNOWLEDGE

"growing in the knowledge of God..." (v 10).

Whatever your Sunday services and small groups look like right now, ask God to help you to continue to grow in your knowledge of him. Pray that during this season, when life has a different pace, members of your church would develop good habits of personal Bible reading and prayer that last for years to come.

ENDURANCE

"being strengthened with all power according to his glorious might so that you may have great endurance and patience..." (v 11).

Pray that your church will grow in patience in this time—perhaps God will use it to prepare you to suffer for Christ in years to come. Pray by name for any believers who you know are struggling spiritually; ask God to strengthen their faith and help them endure.

 JOY

"giving joyful thanks to the Father..." (v 12).

Praise God that he has "qualified you to share in the inheritance of his holy people in the kingdom of light" (v 12). As so many of the other things we enjoy are stripped away, pray that you and your church would have a deepening sense of joy in and gratitude for your guaranteed, unloseable heavenly inheritance.

 NUMBER

"He has rescued us from the dominion of darkness and brought us into the kingdom of the Son he loves, in whom we have redemption, the forgiveness of sins" (v 13-14).

Ask God to work through this crisis to rescue many more people in your community from their sin. Pray that one day soon you would have the joy of gathering together to worship his Son once again.

PRAYING FOR MY CHURCH

ON A SUNDAY

ROMANS 1 v 8-17

PRAYER POINTS:

_____

_____

_____

_____

Father, in this time of separation, help us to…

 ## GIVE THANKS FOR EACH OTHER

"I thank my God through Jesus Christ for all of you, because your faith is being reported all over the world" (v 8).

Thank God for your local church—that, through faith in Jesus Christ, he has made you into a family. Then praise God for the global church—that "all over the world" Christians are waking up to worship him.

 ## LONG FOR EACH OTHER

"I pray that now at last by God's will the way may be opened for me to come to you. I long to see you…" (v 10-11).

Pray that this time of separation would increase your church family's love for one another: that for as long as you "gather" virtually in separate homes, you would be longing for the day when you can be gathered properly, in the flesh. Repent of the times when you have taken that privilege for granted, and ask God to open the way for your church to meet again soon.

ENCOURAGE EACH OTHER

"… that you and I may be mutually encouraged by each other's faith" (v 12).

Thank God for all the ways we are able to keep in touch with one another. On this Lord's day, pray for the Lord to direct you to call and speak to one particular person from your church. Pray for a good conversation about the things of God, and that you would both be encouraged and sharpened.

 ## LISTEN TO YOU

"I am so eager to preach the gospel also to you who are in Rome" (v 15).

As God's word goes out online, pray that your pastor would be eager to preach and that you would be eager to listen! Pray that each element of your "service" would faithfully declare the gospel. Why? Because…

 ## REMEMBER YOUR POWER

"I am not ashamed of the gospel, because it is the power of God that brings salvation to everyone who believes" (v 16).

Praise God that the power of salvation is not in slick livestreams but in faithful gospel proclamation. Praise God that he is powerful enough to preserve the faith of each one of his sheep during this time of separation. Pray that even today there would be those who hear and believe it for the first time, and so are saved.

PRAYING FOR MY CHURCH

MY CHURCH LEADERS

2 TIMOTHY 2 v 1-10

PRAYER POINTS:

_____

_____

_____

_____

 STRENGTH IN GOD'S GRACE

*"You then, my son, be strong in the grace
that is in Christ Jesus" (v 1).*

Praise God that salvation is all by grace. We don't have to earn it, and we don't need to prove ourselves—we simply receive the free gift of righteousness in Christ. Thank God for the way he has saved your church leaders and for the specific gifts he has blessed them with. Pray that they would be conscious of, and find their confidence in, God's grace today.

 GOOD TEAMWORK

*"The things you have heard me say in the
presence of many witnesses entrust to reliable people who will also be qualified to
teach others" (v 2).*

Thank God for the "reliable people" who have a teaching role in your church (staff, elders, small-group leaders, kids' group teachers, etc). Pray for clear communication, mutual trust and gospel unity among them—so that as they work together (even if apart), God's people will be taught, cared for and encouraged.

3 WISE PRIORITIES

"No one serving as a soldier gets entangled in civilian affairs, but rather tries to please his commanding officer" (v 4).

There are probably any number of valid concerns competing for the attention of your pastor(s) right now—as well as a whole bunch of distractions. Pray that day by day, their greatest desire and deepest motivation would be to please the Lord Jesus (v 4)—and that this would help them to make wise decisions about how they spend their time, and about when it's time to rest.

4 CONFIDENCE IN GOD'S WORD

"Remember Jesus Christ, raised from the dead, descended from David. This is my gospel, for which I am suffering even to the point of being chained like a criminal. But God's word is not chained" (v 8-9).

Praise God that even if we are confined, his word is not! Whatever the method of delivery, pray that your church's teaching would keep Jesus Christ central.

5 SALVATION FOR MANY

"Therefore I endure everything for the sake of the elect, that they too may obtain the salvation that is in Christ Jesus" (v 10).

Pray that as your leaders work hard for the sake of your church, the result would be that many souls would come to, and keep clinging to, salvation in Christ.

PRAYING FOR MY CHURCH

VULNERABLE
PEOPLE

3 JOHN v 1-4

PRAYER POINTS:

_____

_____

_____

_____

Use this to pray for a vulnerable member of your church, for whom getting sick might be serious.

DEAR FRIEND

> *"To my dear friend Gaius, whom I love in the truth" (v 1).*

Thank God for this "dear friend". Praise the Lord that the truth of the gospel has knitted you and them together as family; and for the work of his Spirit, who helps you to love one another.

GOOD HEALTH

> *"I pray that you may enjoy good health and that all may go well with you" (v 2).*

Ask God to protect this dear friend from infection and to keep them in good health—both physically and mentally. Think about some of the other practical concerns that they may be facing, and ask God to overrule with his sovereign hand to ensure that they would receive their daily bread—that God would meet their physical needs and their emotional ones as well.

SPIRITUAL PROGRESS

"… just as you are progressing spiritually"
(v 2).

Pray that this season of isolation would be a time of real spiritual progress for your friend. Pray that they would come out the other side abounding in the fruit of the Spirit: love, joy, peace, forbearance, kindness, goodness, faithfulness, gentleness and self-control.

 ## FAITHFULNESS TO THE TRUTH

"It gave me great joy when some believers came and testified about your faithfulness to the truth, telling how you continue to walk in it" (v 3).

In what ways have you witnessed this friend's faithfulness as a Christian, either recently or in the past? Rejoice before God now! Then pray that your friend would continue to be faithful. Pray that they would diligently read God's truth day by day in the Bible, and that as they do, they would love, trust and obey it.

 ## GREAT JOY

"I have no greater joy than to hear that my children are walking in the truth" (v 4).

Just as this person's faithfulness brings you joy, pray that the faith and love of the church would bring them joy too. Ask God to encourage them with stories and memories of brothers and sisters and children in Christ who are "walking in the truth".

PRAYING FOR KINGDOM GROWTH

IN MY COMMUNITY

ACTS 28 v 28-31

PRAYER POINTS:

_____

_____

_____

_____

Father, as we witness in our community, help us to…

REJOICE IN GOD'S SALVATION

"God's salvation has been sent to the Gentiles, and they will listen!" (v 28).

You are living proof of the truth of this verse. So praise God for his salvation through Christ! Thank God that the gospel is for anyone from any background, and that he wants people in your community to hear it. Pray that many would listen and believe.

WELCOME OTHERS

"For two whole years Paul stayed [in Rome] in his own rented house and welcomed all who came to see him" (v 30).

Paul was stuck under house arrest in Rome for *two whole years*. But rather than grow impatient and frustrated with his confinement, he made the most of it for ministry. Pray for inspiration and insight to do the same. Ask God to help you to reach out in friendship to non-Christian friends and neighbours, and to gladly welcome the questions of the spiritually curious.

PROCLAIM BOLDLY

"He proclaimed the kingdom of God ... with all boldness" (v 31).

Pray that this urgent and unusual situation would give Christians in your community renewed boldness in your evangelism. Ask God to show you who he is calling you to courageously share Christ with today—and how.

 **TEACH FAITHFULLY**

"... and taught about the Lord Jesus Christ" (v 31).

Pray for all those Bible teachers you know who have had to adapt to a new way of doing things: pastors, parents, small-group leaders and others. Pray that whatever else has changed, they would keep their message fixed on the same thing and the main thing: the Lord Jesus Christ. Pray that as your church grows in love for their King, you would be more excited to share his kingdom with others.

 WATCH GOD WORK

"... and without hindrance!" (v 31).

Thank God that whatever appearances suggest, no situation is a hindrance to the spread of his gospel. Pray that in his perfect timing, the Lord would make a way for your church to meet and reach out together again; and that when you do, you would be joined by many new believers.

PRAYING FOR KINGDOM GROWTH

AROUND THE WORLD

REVELATION 7 v 9-17

PRAYER POINTS:

_____

_____

_____

_____

 A GREAT MULTITUDE

"I looked, and there before me was a great multitude that no one could count, from every nation, tribe, people and language, standing before the throne" (v 9).

Praise God that this promise *will* come true. He is in the business of bringing people from every nation to worship his Son—and no virus can stop him. Praise God that, by faith, you too will be among that crowd!

 A WISE GOD

"Praise and glory and wisdom and thanks and honour and power and strength be to our God for ever and ever" (v 12).

In his infinite wisdom and power, God does things differently than how our limited vision would suggest he should. Thank him that we can therefore be confident that he will use this situation to achieve his purposes. Pray that as a result of this crisis, more people around the world would give the one true God the praise and glory that is his due. *Then pray for brothers and sisters in specific nations where…*

CHRISTIANS SUFFER

"These are they who have come out of the great tribulation" (v 14).

For many Christians, danger is normal; for many churches, it's always hard to meet. Pray for them—that as suffering intensifies, God would continue to sustain them and keep them speaking of Jesus.

 ## CHRISTIANS HUNGER

"Never again will they hunger; never again will they thirst" (v 16).

In many countries, the effects of this crisis will be compounded by poverty and poor healthcare. Pray for governments and hospitals, churches and charities as they seek to steward very limited resources. And pray that wherever they live, God's people, including you, would be generous with our resources in this life, because we trust God's promises for the next.

 ## CHRISTIANS WEEP

"'He will lead them to springs of living water.' 'And God will wipe away every tear from their eyes'" (v 17).

Pray for Christians around the world who are experiencing sorrow, sickness or grief as a result of this crisis. Ask that they would know the very real comfort of "the Lamb" who is "their shepherd" (v 17); and that their gospel hope in the midst of heartache would be a powerful witness to those around them.

PRAYING FOR KINGDOM GROWTH

AFTER THE PANDEMIC

MATTHEW 9 v 35-38

PRAYER POINTS:

_____

_____

_____

_____

What will life look like after this pandemic? We don't know. But we do know what we should pray for…

 GOOD NEWS

> *"Jesus went through all the town and villages … proclaiming the good news of the kingdom and healing every disease" (v 35).*

Jesus didn't just come to give us a passing glimpse of his perfect kingdom, which is free from disease; he came to open up a way for us to enter it eternally. Praise God that this is indeed "good news"!

 SPIRITUAL SIGHT

> *"When he saw the crowds, he had compassion on them, because they were harassed and helpless…" (v 36).*

Most of us have recently had a taste of feeling "harassed" by circumstances, and helpless to change them and to make life work as we'd like it to. Pray that as post-crisis life goes back to normal for most people, they would not revert to feeling self-sufficient but would have their eyes opened to their spiritual need.

FRESH COMPASSION

"… like sheep without a shepherd" (v 36).

Pray that you and all God's people would be moved by fresh compassion to speak of your Good Shepherd to others. Thank Jesus for the way he laid down his life for his sheep; pray for specific people you know to come to understand the sacrifice of the cross. Pray that they'd experience the joy and security that comes from following the Good Shepherd.

 A PLENTIFUL HARVEST

"The harvest is plentiful…" (v 37).

The long-term economic outlook may prove to be bleak—but praise God that the spiritual outlook is "plentiful"! Whatever your concerns for the future, ask him to encourage your soul with the truth that he is at work to call many people to himself.

 MORE WORKERS

"… but the workers are few. Ask the Lord of the harvest, therefore, to send out workers into his harvest field" (v 37-38).

Ask this now! Pray that one result of this crisis would be a generation of Christians who are recommitted and ready to put their hand to the sickle in God's harvest field. After months with much of life "on hold", pray that you and your church would move forward with renewed faith and fresh momentum as you seek to proclaim the good news to your community.

DISCOVER THE SERIES:

We all want to pray and know it's important, but our prayer lives can get stuck in a rut.

These books will give you lots of ideas when you don't know what to pray. Each page takes a passage of Scripture and suggests five things to pray for the people and places you care about. Because when we pray in line with God's priorities as found in his word, our prayers are powerful—they really change things.

THEGOODBOOK.CO.UK/5THINGS
THEGOODBOOK.COM/5THINGS

BIBLICAL | RELEVANT | ACCESSIBLE

At The Good Book Company, we are dedicated to helping Christians and local churches grow. We believe that God's growth process always starts with hearing clearly what he has said to us through his timeless word—the Bible.

Ever since we opened our doors in 1991, we have been striving to produce Bible-based resources that bring glory to God. We have grown to become an international provider of user-friendly resources to the Christian community, with believers of all backgrounds and denominations using our books, Bible studies, devotionals, evangelistic resources, and DVD-based courses.

We want to equip ordinary Christians to live for Christ day by day, and churches to grow in their knowledge of God, their love for one another, and the effectiveness of their outreach.

Call us for a discussion of your needs or visit one of our local websites for more information on the resources and services we provide.

Your friends at The Good Book Company

thegoodbook.com | thegoodbook.co.uk
thegoodbook.com.au | thegoodbook.co.nz
thegoodbook.co.in